The
Waldorf
Kindergarten
Snack Book

Collected and Annotated by Lisa Hildreth
Illustrated by Jo Valens

BELL POND BOOKS

Published by Bell Pond Books
610 Main Street
Great Barrington, Massachusetts 01230

www.bellpondbooks.com

10 9 8 7 6 5 4

Library of Congress Cataloging-in-Publication Data

Hildreth, Lisa.
  The Waldorf kindergarten snack book / collected and annotated by Lisa Hildreth;
illustrated by Jo Valens.— 1st ed.
    p. cm.
  ISBN 978-0-88010-563-7
1. Snack foods. 2. Cookery. I. Title.

TX740.H55 2005
641.5'39—dc22

                      2005027509

Contents

Acknowledgements

This book is the result of the work of many different Waldorf kindergarten teachers who generously helped me by sharing their snack menus, recipes, and thoughts on food. It also reflects a bit of my own journey as a teacher, as I experienced the classrooms and food at the Green Meadow Waldorf School (as an assistant), the Great Barrington Rudolf Steiner School (as a regular substitute), and the Susquehanna Waldorf School (as a lead teacher).

Please note that I have kept all the menus, recipes, and teachers' names and schools just as they were when they first shared their thoughts with me. Of course, since then, teachers have changed their menus, their schools, and some have even changed their names! Life never stands still.

I hope you all find this book an enjoyable and useful addition to your Waldorf book collection. Thank you!

Lisa Hildreth
July 2005
Lancaster, Pennsylvania

Abbreviations Used in this Cookbook

t. = teaspoon
T. = Tablespoon

1. Planning Your Snacks

This chapter discusses some of the things you may wish to consider when you are planning your snack menu. It considers questions such as:

- How are snacks a part of our day?
- What foods nourish young children?
- How does food affect the process of incarnation?
- What foods might you wish to avoid?
- What about sugar?
- What types of snacks will you decide to offer?
- How can snacks help children make connections?
- Will the snacks meet the needs of your special group of children?

How Are Snacks a Part of Our Day?

In the Waldorf kindergarten, snacks are not only an important activity of the day, but they *are* the day! For example, in my classroom, we have soup day, bread day, porridge day, applesauce day, and popcorn day.

When deciding how the snacks will fit into your daily rhythm, you may wish to consider the following questions:

• *How involved will the children be in the snack preparation?* Let's say that you are making bread. Will you prepare the dough before the children arrive, or with the children? Will you require all the children to knead the dough at the same time, or will you invite only a few at a time to the kneading table while the others play? Are the children always going to be involved with the snack preparation, or on certain days will the teachers make the snack before they arrive?

• *How can you balance snack preparation with the other activities of the day?* If you are planning to do an involved activity on a certain day, such as painting, you may wish to balance it with a simple snack. For example, at the Great Barrington Rudolf Steiner School an assistant teacher makes popcorn (before the children arrive) for the snack on painting day. Similarly, some kindergartens make oatmeal or eat bread that they baked on a previous day.

What Foods Nourish Young Children?

When I was gathering information for this book, I asked teachers what their thinking was behind selecting their snacks. Their answers speak to this question about the kind of food we, as kindergarten teachers, wish to offer our children:

"Nutritious, whole grains, fresh produce, protein."

"Using whole grains and letting the children participate in the preparation as much as possible."

"I selected snacks with whole grains and vegetables, primarily because I believe they are a staple of life."

"whole grains, whole foods, varied..."

The following thoughts offer some insights into what nourishes the young child:

• *What are whole foods and why are they important?* Whole foods are the food just as it is given to us by nature. For example, an apple is a whole food.

Of course, we don't always eat our foods this way; generally we subject them to some kind of processing before eating them. For example, we may eat our apples as home-cooked applesauce (apples processed by warmth) or may grind our wheat into flour for our bread. The problem occurs when foods become *over processed*. For example, consider the processing required to convert wheat grains (the whole food) into the dough for a grocery-store donut (the processed food):

wheat grain
grind it
↓
whole wheat flour
remove bran and germ and bleach it
↓
white flour
add vitamins and preservatives
↓
enriched, brominated flour
add yeast, dough conditioners, preservatives, and other ingredients
↓
dough for donut

If you compare the grain to the finished product, you can see that most of the original food value is gone and only "empty" calories remain. Therefore it is important to be conscious of just how much processing has occurred to our food and how much nutritional value has been lost.

• *What other factors affect the quality of food?* Was the produce grown on a conventional farm using chemical fertilizers and insecticides? Or was it grown on a organic or biodynamic farm where no chemicals are used and care is taken to maintain the health, mineral content, and vitality of the soil? According to Dr. Glöckler, the type of conditions in which a plant or animal is raised can greatly affect the quality of the food. For example:

"Radishes and spinach forced on by nitrogen fertilizers have a high water content, taste more insipid than those not so fertilized, do not keep so well, have a higher nitrate content (spinach) and show atypical growth tendencies..." (*A Guide to Child Health*, pg. 246).

Similarly, there is a difference in the nutritional value of freshly harvested foods and stored foods, fresh foods being preferred.

Even the way the food is stored can affect the produce. For example, the starch content of the potato increases with cold storage.

Because of the ways in which these factors affect the quality of the food we are eating, the best solution may be to seek out a local organic or biodynamic farm — one where you can talk to the farmer about how he or she grows and stores the food offered.

• *What foods should pre-school children be eating?* In *A Guide to Child Health*, Dr. Glöckler recommends:

– cow's *milk* (and other dairy products) — the fresher the better
– *butter* — as the principal fat for children (other cold pressed oils, such as olive oil or sunflower oil may be used)
– more *grain* in the diet (be careful not to add too much)
– *vegetables* and lettuce
– *fruit*
– *eggs, meat, and fish* (after the end of the third year, if desired by the child) (pgs. 249-257).

She also notes that although she recommends a lacto-vegetable diet (dairy, grains, fruits, and vegetables) for the first three years of a child's life, in later childhood the child's diet should be "suited to the individual's need, varied, of the best available quality, with not too much protein" (pg. 257). However, children still need to eat balanced diets, even if their appetite is not balanced. If the children find certain foods unappealing, Dr. Glöckler suggests that the cook needs to work on preparing the food in a way that is appetizing to the child. Maybe it is overcooked or too bitter for the child's taste. Sometimes disguising the unwanted food in a blend of other foods can help (pg. 253).

How Does Food Affect the Process of Incarnation?

In her book, *The Incarnating Child*, Joan Salter speaks about how different foods affect the child's growing consciousness in different ways. Working out of the insights provided by Dr. Steiner, Salter suggests the following progression of foods for the baby and young child:

1. *Mother's milk* — Human milk contains a spiritual quality, and this "natural, welcoming food, more than anything else, guides the child to earth, and at the same time keeps him in touch with the wider cosmos" (pg. 58).

2. *At about 6 months, fruits such as apples, pears, and stoned fruit* —These fruits hang above the earth, on a stem that is so thin that they hardly seem connected. Moreover, fruit blossoms are pollinated by bees, which Rudolf Steiner, in his lecture on bees, describes as "living in an atmosphere completely pervaded by love." Steiner relates "the whole wonderful activity within the hive to the life of love, to that part of life connected with the planet Venus. The bees, as creatures of love and soul, bestow upon the blossom the gift of the higher life of soul" (pg. 62).

3. *Oatmeal porridge, followed by millet, rice, and ground wheat* — The grains, unlike fruits, do not contain a soul element, rather, they can be looked at in relationship to the elements: oats to fire, wheat to solid earth, rye to heaviness of water, barley to air. Rice is connected to water and light, and has helped the people of the East remain more oriented to the spirit than to the physical (pg. 63).

4. *At about 7 months, cooked vegetables*—Vegetables help the child to connect with the earth, gently. Begin with those that grow above the ground, followed by those that grow below (pg. 65).

5. *At 1 year, fresh milk and then yogurt and cottage or ricotta cheese* — "In the cow, nature and earth forces are inextricably woven together" (pg. 67). However, the milk of the cow expresses these animal and earth forces more weakly than cow meat. Therefore it "helps to bring the child into incarnation in an appropriate way, not anchoring him too firmly in earth forces at an early age" (pg. 67).

6. *After the first birthday, a little chicken or fish may be added to the diet* — Chickens (as birds) belong to the air element and fish to the water element, making them appropriate meats for children, *if you wish to introduce meat before age 7* (pg. 66).

7. *After age 3, one or two eggs a week may be added to the diet* — Eggs carry a strong fertility impulse; they can bring in the puberty forces at too young an age (pg. 67).

In conclusion, Salter shares:

"As the child grows older, diet is a matter of good-quality food and common sense. *It should never be a matter of fanaticism.* The baby becomes a toddler and can share the family meal within reason. A greater variety of foods can be introduced — dried fruits, wheat germ, herbs such as mints, marjoram, thyme and rosemary which have a warming effect on the digestive tract, a variety of breads such as rye which is a good form of protein, later nuts, and later still as we have seen, eggs and peas and beans." (pg. 70).

What Foods Might You Wish to Avoid?

According to Dr. Glöckler (in *A Guide to Child Health*), the following foods may not be appropriate for the pre-school child:

• *Margarine and hard fats* — such as lard (pg. 250).

• *High-fiber foods, coarse meal, and unground seeds* — These foods provide too much cellulose for the children's digestive systems (pg. 251).

• *Potatoes* — According to Rudolf Steiner, these tubers tend to suppress meditative thinking and encourage sense-oriented, materialistic thinking. In addition, potatoes tend to be addictive and can weaken the mid-brain area for children and the eyes in old age (pg. 252).

• *Bananas* — The number of bananas eaten should be limited. "Bananas contain good nourishment but not much vitalizing force. They are very filling but they do make the system rather sluggish. Furthermore the process used in harvesting and storing the unripe fruit leaves a lot to be desired" (pg. 253).

• *White and brown sugar* (pg. 255).

• *Salty foods* — Generally, the children's bread and milk products contain enough salt for the child's diet (pg. 257).

Joan Salter, in *The Incarnating Child*, suggests avoiding several other foods:

• *Nightshades (tomatoes, peppers, eggplant, also potatoes)* — "The normal protein forming process in the seed, takes the abnormal course of making alkaloids, and the nightshades have an above-average nitrogen content. As adults with an ego fully incarnated, we are able to deal with this influence, but for a child whose ego is in the process of incarnation and body building, it is a different matter" (pg. 69).

• *Red meat* — Meat pulls the child too quickly into the material realm and weakens his connections to the spiritual world (pg. 66).

• *Mushrooms* — They are a fungus that grows in strong connection to the earth, without taking in the sun forces (pg. 69).

However, when speaking about these foods, Dr. Glöckler cautions us to be aware of a common misunderstanding:

"namely that, from an anthroposophical point of view, certain foods are recommended or forbidden. Rudolf Steiner always emphasized that he would not take sides for or against any particular food, and that he would only offer points of view which would enable others to make a more consciously selected diet." (pg. 248).

It is in this same spirit that these lists of "recommended" and "forbidden" foods are offered in this cookbook.

What about Sugar?

Sugar is a hidden ingredient that appears in so many processed food items. When I see the "healthy" food that many parents put in their young child's lunch, I am amazed at the amount of sugar it contains. For example, much of the peanut butter, jelly, yogurt, apple sauce, fruit leathers, breakfast bars, granola bars, and canned fruit that is in the lunch boxes contains sugar and/or corn syrup as an ingredient. All this sugar comes to school, even when policies state that lunches should not contain desserts, juices, or other sugary foods!

So what about sugar? Is it all bad, or does it have a useful place in our diet? In *A Guide to Child Health*, Dr. Glöckler says that sweetness:

"comforts, consoles, calms and supports. It immediately strengthens our feeling of self, making us feel stronger and better in our bodies. This effect awakens the desire for more sugar. We enjoy the momentary increase in strength and do not notice the ensuing decline in strength which we seek to compensate for by an even greater sugar consumption." (pg. 254).

As you can see, parents and teachers need to be very conscious of just how much sugar the children in their care are consuming. However, in moderation, sugar can be very important for the human being, especially during sickness when the body cannot properly carry out its own digestion (pg. 254). Also, sugar can play a part in helping to balance the temperament of melancholic children. Rudolf Steiner recommended letting these children have more sugar in their diet, to normalize their liver function. On the other hand, sanguine children often crave carbohydrates and sweets, and Rudolf Steiner often recommended reducing the amount of sugar in their diet (*Education as Preventive Medicine*, pg. 162).

But what kind of sugar, in moderation, is best for young children? As mentioned previously, Dr. Glöckler does not recommend white or brown sugar. What other options are there?

• *Natural Cane Sugars* — Rapadura and Sucanat are natural cane sugars made of evaporated cane juice. Unlike white sugar, these products are minimally processed (the juice is extracted, evaporated, and the remaining sugar is simply chopped up) and they retain the nutrients and minerals of the sugar cane. Dr. Glöckler prefers this type of sugar over white or brown sugar (pg. 256).

• *Molasses* — A "waste" product from the sugar production process, molasses can contain many minerals, such as iron, calcium, zinc, copper, and chromium. However, it has a strong flavor and does not work well in all recipes (*Nourishing Traditions*, pg. 537). Molasses is also recommended for young children by Dr. Glöckler (pg. 255).

• *Maple Syrup* — From the boiled sap of the sugar maple trees, maple sugar is rich in trace minerals. It adds a wonderful flavor to most baked goods. However, formaldehyde is used in the production of most commercial maple syrups so you may wish to consider using organic maple syrup (*Nourishing Traditions*, pg. 536). Maple syrup is not mentioned by Dr. Glöckler.

• *Honey* — A gift from the bees to humanity, honey is so much more than just another "natural" sugar. In fact, Dr. Glöckler says that honey should *not* be used as a sweetener, for it is has an effect similar to a medicine on the human body (pg. 256). Joan Salter, in *The Incarnating Child*, also speaks of the special nature of honey. She describes it as a "living food" containing a "variety of

formative forces" (pg. 68). Ms. Salter also speaks of how Rudolf Steiner identified honey as an ideal food for older people "when restorative forces of the ego are waning; and more than any other food, honey helps us to be orientated towards higher realms of existence" (pg. 68). Therefore, Rudolf Steiner advised that honey should not be given to very young children, or if it is given, it should be in very small amounts. For as milk helps the young child incarnate on this earth, honey helps the old reorient themselves to the non-earthly realms, as they prepare to return to the spiritual world (pg. 68).

• *Malted Grain Syrups* — Used for thousands of years (especially in the Orient), these syrups are often made from malted barley grains. They contain only small amounts of nutrients (*Nourishing Traditions*, pg. 537). Malted grain syrups are not mentioned by Dr. Glöckler.

What Types of Snacks will You Decide to Offer?

The snacks that we offer in our classroom are only a small part of what the children eat each day. However, it can be one way to move the children toward a new way of eating.

When you are choosing your snacks, consider the following questions:

• *What "new" foods will you introduce to the children?* The snacks you choose to provide may contain a number of foods that the children are not familiar with. Is this a problem? — No. To quote an experienced teacher, "the children almost invariably come around to eating and *enjoying* all the foods in spite of any antipathies at first."

And another teacher, "Children will eat healthy foods if you don't discuss the fact that it is healthy; my children have eaten combinations of millet, barley, and spelt ravenously."

• *What foods have you decided to avoid?* I think this is a question that bears consideration in advance. For example, do you think it is acceptable to use sugar in the birthday muffins? What will you do on vegetable soup day when a parent sends noodles instead of a vegetable? Will you include the noodles in the soup, or will you decide, like the teachers at the Great Barrington Rudolf Steiner School, that the children are already eating enough wheat and that you want vegetables to be the main focus of your snack? Obviously, you cannot predict all the food decisions you will need to make during the year. But it may be a help to decide what your food goals are now.

• *What types of eating habits are you trying to create?* A father at the Great Barrington Rudolf Steiner School joked with one of the teachers that after 3 years of eating porridge on Monday mornings, his daughter would probably want porridge on Mondays for the rest of her life... even on business trips! We all had a good laugh. But then I started thinking — how are we creating habits with our snacks?

• *Do you want to provide a warm snack every day?* If we are trying to provide a warm and loving atmosphere in the kindergarten, doesn't it make sense to provide a warm snack as well? Warm snacks seem especially soothing in the fall and winter. But what about in the spring? I have noticed that some teachers switch from soup to fruit salad when the weather warms up. What do you think?

• *How full do you want the children to be from their snack?* Some types of food fill the children's tummies more than others. For example, on bread day, my own two children were never hungry at lunch time. I always had to postpone lunch for an hour or two. Then later, as a teacher, I noticed that in the afternoon children also ate very little lunch on bread day. However, popcorn for snack had the opposite effect; my children were always starving at lunch time. So how filling are your snacks? And how many helpings will you allow the children to have?

How Can Snacks Help Children Make Connections?

I think most people will agree that it is much harder for the children of today to make connections with the natural world. And technology like televisions and computers take them even further away from reality.

So how can snacks in the kindergarten help? We can try our best to let the child experience as much of the food growing, preparation, and cooking process as possible. For example, compare the experience of opening a jar of applesauce and eating it to the experience of going to the orchard, picking the apples, cleaning and chopping them, stirring the cooking pot, and then eating the applesauce!

However, not every connection in the kindergarten needs to be a whole field trip. For example, Annamay Keeney from the Waldorf School of Atlanta shared with me that 3 of her children regularly asked her what was for snack today just after they had all finished chopping vegetables and cleaning up! After letting them pour the chopped vegetables into the hot soup pot, they have not asked since.

The following are some thoughts to consider:

• *What can you grow or raise with the children and then eat as part of your snack?* Since few of our children grow up on a farm and many even do not have a family garden, it is increasingly important that education helps the children understand where our food comes from. When they visit the grocery store, the food is all laid out in front of them. But there is no hint of the miracle and hard work that lies behind it. Could your children plant, hoe, water, and harvest some peas, lettuce, radishes, or another spring vegetable? Could you raise chickens or visit a farm that does, collect the eggs, and then cook them for snack? Could you have an herb garden and grow and dry the herbs for your tea?

• *Will your snacks follow a cosmic or seasonal rhythm?* Many teachers I spoke to have chosen to follow the cosmic rhythm of the daily grain (see the "A Grain a Day" chapter for more information). Others enjoy using seasonal vegetables in their soups (for example, root vegetables and winter squashes in the winter). A few even stop making soup when the weather becomes warm and switch to fruit salad.

• *Do you want to include "community" snacks in your menu?* (By community snacks, I mean snacks like stone soup or applesauce, where each child contributes their own vegetable or fruit to the pot.) Many children enjoy picking out that special vegetable to bring to class and even try to find pieces of "their" vegetable in their soup bowl. It is another way of creating connections to the food they prepare and eat.

• *Could your kindergarten cook or bake for others in your school or community?* Can you create some connections with the people around you? For example, Viorica

Comaniciu of The River Valley School shared that her kindergarten class made soup for the 2nd grade and bread for the 1st grade. All year long, she says, these two grades enjoyed the good smells from the nearby kindergarten classes, and they had some good food too. Susan Howard of Sunbridge College spoke of a kindergarten class in a very small school that makes soup for the other children and faculty at their school.

Will the Snacks Meet the Needs of Your Special Group of Children?

As you well know, each group of children you teach is unique, and the snacks that you served last year might not suit these new children. What should you adjust? The following are some questions to consider:

• *Do your children need a snack before snack time?* Increasingly, it seems, teachers are finding that children are too hungry to wait until snack time. Often this empty-tummy feeling shows up as behavioral problems or with simply asking again and again for something to eat. Different teachers have developed their own ways of handling this situation — some have a tea time *before* snack time, others provide "mousie nibbles" or a "little gnomes' snack" before circle, and others have moved their snack time earlier in the day. Types of foods offered as nibbles include nuts, chunks of cheese, crackers, and pieces of fruits or vegetables (such as carrot rounds or apple wedges).

• *What about breakfast?* Did you ever think of providing a simple porridge breakfast for hungry parents or children? Susan Howard has observed this type of breakfast in a couple of Waldorf schools, particularly in Parent/Toddler classes. The breakfast was informal; parents and children were invited to have a bowl of porridge when they arrived. But something as simple as porridge can send a powerful message — I have what will nourish you. Similarly, Heather Cohill of the Waldorf School of Baltimore found that many of her children were hungry when they arrived in the morning. So she began to provide her children with oatbars as their school breakfast. (See the "A Grain a Day" chapter for the recipe for oatbars.)

• *Have you considered increasing the amount of protein in your snacks?* Several teachers I spoke to have added more protein items (such as almonds and cheese) to their snacks. They feel that their children were more grounded and focused after they added these foods to their snack menus. In some cases, these protein items were given to the children as part of their "mousie nibbles" earlier in the morning.

• *How will you alter your snack to meet the needs of children with allergies?* For example, what happens if you normally put butter on your freshly-baked rolls and this year you have a child who is allergic to dairy? Will you provide a different spread for that child only (and therefore single him or her out)? Will you change to something else, like almond butter, that all the children can have?

My Notes

2. Snack Menus

Haven't you always wondered what other Waldorf kindergarten teachers make and eat at their snack time? I certainly did when I began teaching.

Here are some of the snack menus I collected. I think these provide a good "picture" of snack time in Waldorf kindergartens (in the USA).

Please remember that not all nursery and kindergarten classes in the same school serve the same snacks. Also note that teachers often adjust their menus from year to year.

If an item in the menu is marked with a asterisk (*), the recipe is included in this book.

3-Day Nursery Menus

Monday	rolls* with butter (see Very Easy Bread recipe)
Tuesday	oatmeal porridge* with maple syrup
Wednesday	vegetable soup

Shared by Jill Farrell ~
Green Meadow Waldorf School, New York

Tuesday	rice cakes with peanut butter, raisins
Wednesday	rye crackers with butter, soynuts
Thursday	tortilla chips and salsa, sesame sticks
Beverage:	wildberry zinger tea (unsweetened) and water

Shared by Lise Stoessel ~
Charlottesville Waldorf School, Virginia

*Here is an example of how a healthy snack may be provided even if your class is at a site that is controlled by Health Department and Daycare regulations and **you cannot cook or wash dishes**! Teachers at this site are also required to use prepackaged foods and serve more than one food group each day.*

5-Day Kindergarten Menus

Monday	rice with tamari and butter
Tuesday	oatmeal porridge with butter and maple syrup
Wednesday	millet with tamari and butter
Thursday	bread with butter
Friday	stone soup with barley

Shared by Linda Kenney ~
Charlottesville Waldorf School, Virginia

Monday	rice porridge* with maple syrup (bake bread for week)
Tuesday	vegetable soup* with toasted bread (croutons)
Wednesday	bread with almond butter
Thursday	millet squares* and apple/pear sauce*
Friday	popcorn*

Shared by Diane Prusha ~
Great Barrington Rudolf Steiner School,
Massachusetts

Monday	rice with herb salt
Tuesday	oatmeal with maple syrup
Wednesday	millet cakes* with jam
Thursday	stone soup/fruit salad in spring
Friday	bread with butter and jam

Shared by Brooke Redgrave ~
The Pine Tree Room, a Waldorf home care
program in Baltimore, Maryland

Monday   *grain: rice*   *color: purple*
rice cakes, cereal, or pudding
blueberries, plums, or grapes

Tuesday   *grain: oats*   *color: red*
oat bread or muffins
apples or strawberries

Wednesday   *grain: millet*   *color: yellow*
millet
bananas, nuts, or raisins

Thursday   *grain: barley*   *color: orange*
cooked barley or pretzels
cantaloupe, oranges, or carrots

Friday   *grain: rye*   *color: green*
rye crackers and cheese
pears, kiwi, or grapes

Shared by Maryla Sikora ~
Four Winds School, Illionis

Monday	rice with broccoli
Tuesday	apple crisp or bread
Wednesday	vegetable soup
Thursday	stir fry with grain (usually barley)
Friday	oatmeal

Shared by Maryla Sikora ~
Four Winds School, Illionis

Ever thought of joining an organic co-op?
Maryla Sikora's class uses the fruits and
vegetables from their co-op delivery to prepare
these snacks.

Monday	honey muffins*
Tuesday	rolls
Wednesday	vegetable soup and bread
Thursday	popcorn
Friday	carrot cake* or rice cakes with cream cheese

Shared by Carolyn Lin ~
Rudolf Steiner School, New York

Monday	rice porridge with raisins, nuts, and syrup
Tuesday	oatmeal porridge with raisins, nuts, syrup, and cinnamon
Wednesday	Hummus, corn tortilla chips, vegetables (baby carrots, celery, cucumbers)
Thursday	soup with barley, crackers
Friday	baking day: southern cornbread* with butter and jelly; *or a surprise baked item*, such as muffins, scones, or cookies

Shared by Kirsten Carr ~
The Waldorf School, Lexington, Massachusetts

Monday	rice pilaf*
Tuesday	vegetable and barley soup
Wednesday	millet squares* and applesauce
Thursday	bread with honey butter
Friday	muffins

Shared by Ruth Kasl ~
Susquehanna Waldorf School, Pennsylvania

4-Day Kindergarten Menus

Monday	oatmeal, raisins, almonds
Tuesday	bread with peanut butter, sliced apples
Wednesday	rice with melted butter, tamari, and salt; carrot sticks, almonds (children may add gomashio and powdered dulse to rice)
Thursday	stone soup, cheese
Friday	—

Shared by Nancy Segreto ~
Green Mountain Waldorf School, Vermont

Monday	—
Tuesday	vegetable soup with toasted bread (croutons)
Wednesday	rolls* with honey (see Rose Room Rolls recipe)
Thursday	oatmeal with apple/pear sauce*
Friday	flatbread* with almond butter, sliced apples

Shared by Christine Inglis ~
Great Barrington Rudolf Steiner School, Massachusetts

My Menus

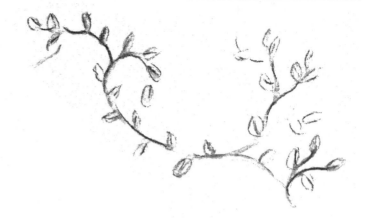

3. Our Daily Bread

Some things seem almost universal in the Waldorf kindergarten, and bread day is one of them. Nothing is quite as satisfying as enjoying homemade bread, fresh from the oven.

This chapter contains several yeasted bread recipes, a non-yeasted flat bread, cornbread recipes, and a biscuit recipe.

Some Stories to Share

The Rose Room at the Great Barrington Rudolf Steiner School makes bread twice a week. For the past couple of years, this class was a 4-day class with a 2-day option. Christine Inglis wanted to make sure all the 2-day children had a chance to work with dough, so their schedule included kneading dough on both Wednesdays and Fridays. One bread is a yeasted roll, the other is a flat bread (no yeast).

The Rudolf Steiner School in New York City does a really big baking. They use part of the dough to make rolls to eat that day. Then the rest of the dough is formed into bread loaves to be enjoyed the following day.

One teacher shared that because of health and daycare regulations, she cannot cook or bake snacks with her children. However, they are allowed to bake bread as a "craft project" and take it home at the end of the morning.

Beautiful Bread

When I started substituting at the Great Barrington Rudolf Steiner School, I was amazed at the beautifully decorated loaves the children were making. After they kneaded the dough, the children were free to make whatever figures or patterns they liked. Older children often rolled the dough into long "snakes" and then braided them. Others created little people or animals. Still others rolled long strips of dough in a spiral form to create roses. Some of these braids, figures, and flowers ended up on the top of the loaf, making the bread not only a wonderful snack, but beautiful as well.

Many teachers make their loaves in special shapes for the different festivals. Please see the "Festival Foods" chapter for a description of some of these fancy loaves.

Dandelion Room's Yummy Bread

1 T. yeast
1/3 cup honey
3 cups warm water (not too hot)
6 cups of flour (3 cups white and 3 cups whole wheat)
1/3 cup oil
1 T. salt

1. Stir together the honey, warm water, and yeast. Wait for it to get foamy.
2. Stir in 3 cups of flour (part white and part whole wheat) and let sit for about 45 minutes to rise.
3. Stir in the remaining 3 cups of flour, the salt, and the oil to form dough.
4. Sprinkle flour on the table and knead the dough until firm.
5. Form dough into rolls and bake at 325° for about 15 minutes.

Shared by Heather Cohill ~
Waldorf School of Baltimore, Maryland

Rose Room Rolls

Served with honey on top.

2 T. yeast
3 cups warm water
2 T. honey
3 T. oil
8 cups of flour (mix of whole wheat and white)

1. Stir together the honey, warm water, and yeast. Wait for it to get foamy.
2. Add the oil and flour and stir until it forms a dough.

3. Knead the dough and form dough into rolls.
4. Let rise for 30 minutes.
5. Bake at 325° for 18 minutes.

Shared by Christine Inglis ~
Great Barrington Rudolf Steiner School, Massachusetts

Flat Bread

A favorite non-yeasted bread at the Great Barrington Rudolf Steiner School. The children refer to this as the "not sticky" bread (as opposed to the sticky yeasted dough). Served with almond butter and sliced apples.

1 cup water
2 T. corn oil
1/2 t. salt
3 to 4 cups of flour (mix of whole wheat and white)

1. Preheat oven to 350°.
2. Mix together all ingredients.
3. Knead dough lightly and form flattened "rolls."
4. Bake for 20 minutes.

Shared by Christine Inglis ~
Great Barrington Rudolf Steiner School, Massachusetts

Very Easy Bread Recipe

Served warm with butter.

2 cups very warm water
large spoonful of honey
1 T. yeast
flour (a mix of white and whole wheat)
1 t. salt

1. Put warm water into a large mixing bowl and stir in honey.
2. Sprinkle the yeast over top of the water. Let it foam up.
3. Start adding flour and sprinkle in the salt. Children love to make it "snow" into the bowl.
4. When the dough is stiff and no longer sticky, cover it with a "blanket" and let it rest for a little while (about 15 minutes).
5. Knead the dough and form dough into rolls.
6. Place rolls on an oiled baking sheet.
7. If you have time, you can let them rise a little longer on the pan, covered.
8. Bake at 350° for about 20 minutes or until light brown.

Shared by Jill Farrell ~
Green Meadow Waldorf School, New York

Skillet Corn Bread

At the Mossy Rock Children's Garden, a home care in Connecticut, Susan grinds the corn for the bread with the children. They always grind extra, to share with the chickens.

3/4 cup whole wheat or white flour
1-1/4 cups cornmeal
2-1/2 t. baking soda

3/4 t. salt
2 to 3 T. butter
1 cup milk
1 egg (beaten)

1. Preheat oven to 350°.
2. Put a 10-inch cast-iron skillet in the oven to heat.
3. In a large bowl, mix the flour, cornmeal, baking soda, and salt.
4. Put butter in the hot skillet to melt.
5. Make a hole in the middle of the dry ingredients.
6. Add milk, egg, and melted butter (swish butter around skillet first before adding to the batter).
7. Mix batter and pour into skillet.
8. Bake for 20 to 25 minutes.

Shared by Susan Lynch ~
Mossy Rock Children's Garden,
Danielson, Connecticut

Biscuits

Arrowhead Mills has a pancake / waffle mix with a biscuit recipe on the side. The children enjoy cutting out the biscuits with seasonal cookie cutters and they love to eat them with butter and honey.

Michaelann suggests using milk instead of water; it makes them fluffier.

Shared by Michaelann Murphy ~
Hawthorne Valley Waldorf School, New York

Southern Corn Bread

Wheat free!
Served with butter and jelly.

1/4 cup oil
3 cups cornmeal
3 t. baking powder
1-1/2 t. baking soda (only if using buttermilk)
1-1/2 t. salt
2 cups buttermilk or soymilk
2 eggs

1. Preheat oven to 375°.
2. Heat oil in frying pan or in a baking pan in the oven.
3. Sift the dry ingredients.
4. In a large bowl, combine the buttermilk and eggs. Then mix into the dry ingredients.
5. Pour oil into the batter and mix in well.
6. Pour batter into pan and bake for 20 to 30 minutes.

Shared by Kirsten Carr ~
The Waldorf School, Lexington, Massachusetts

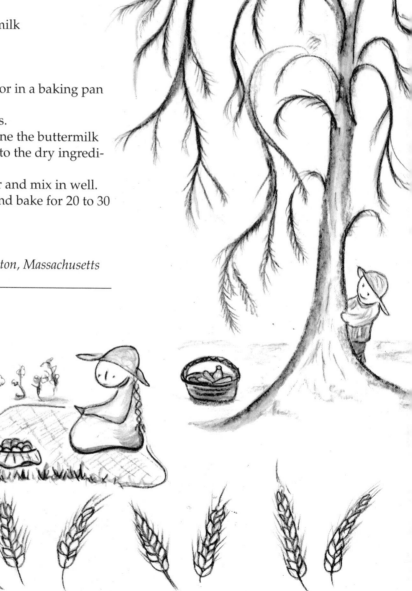

4. Warming Soups

Almost all the teachers I spoke to have a soup day for their class. It seems to be one of the easiest and most pleasing ways to include cooked vegetables in your weekly menu. Many also manage to include the grain of the day in their soup, thus satisfying that goal as well. The most common grain added was barley. Rice or noodles also were included by some teachers.

This chapter contains four variations of Waldorf kindergarten vegetable soup — enough I think to give you some ideas and whet your appetite. It is interesting that all the soups include vegetables brought from home to school by the children — an example of a true *community* snack.

A Stone in My Soup?

Quite a few teachers regularly add a stone or two into their soup pot. I asked them why. Here are some of their stories.

At Green Meadow Waldorf School, the stones in the soup are not just any stones — they are magic, wishing stones! Whoever gets a stone in their bowl can make a special wish. Then they are passed around the table so that each child may make a wish.

Similarly, Brooke Redgrave decided to include a wishing stone in their soup at her Waldorf home care, The Pine Tree Room. She found that soup was the hardest snack

for her children — either because they were not used to the particular vegetables or they didn't like them all mixed together in a soup. They really enjoyed checking their bowl to see if they had the lucky stone and they eventually even learned to like the soup.

Linda Kenney, from the Charlottesville Waldorf School, shares that her children love the stone in their soup. Their stone keeps their soup *warm*. It also brings to mind the "stone soup" story with the hungry soldiers and the soup they made with a little help from everyone in the village.

Stone Soup

One of my son's favorite stories is about how his teacher at Green Meadow Waldorf School, Naomi Olson, got both the wishing stones in her bowl one day. Oops!
~ Lisa Hildreth

olive oil
chopped onions
water
1 vegetable bouillon cube
vegetables brought by the children
2 small, round, river stones

1. In bottom of soup pot, sauté the chopped onions in olive oil.
2. Add several inches of water to the pot and bring to a boil.
3. Add the bouillon cube.
4. With the children's help, chop the vegetables.
5. Add chopped vegetables to the pot. Add more water if needed to cover vegetables.
6. Simmer until tender.
7. Just before serving, add the stones to the soup.

Shared by Lisa Hildreth ~ formerly of Green Meadow Waldorf School, New York

Vegetable Soup

Every Tuesday at the Great Barrington Rudolf Steiner School, the early childhood children come in laden with their vegetable offerings. The variety is amazing and no matter what comes, the soup is always delicious. Christine Zelehoski once told me that she tried to duplicate the soup at home for her family, but never could.
~ Lisa Hildreth

Served with toasted bread squares (croutons) on the side.

olive oil
chopped onions
water
vegetables brought by the children
salt

1. In bottom of soup pot, sauté the chopped onions in olive oil.
2. With the children's help, chop all the vegetables.
3. Sauté the chopped vegetables in the oil for a couple of minutes.
4. Add water to cover vegetables and bring to a boil.
5. Add salt and simmer over medium heat for about 1/2 hour or until tender.

Croutons

Cut bread slices into quarters. Spread out in roasting pan and toast in the oven at 200° for 30 minutes.

Shared by Diane Prusha ~ Great Barrington Rudolf Steiner School, Massachusetts

Dandelion Room Soup

butter
1 onion, chopped
1 clove garlic, minced
water
spices (such as oregano, basil, and paprika)
lentils
vegetables brought by the children
noodles (optional)

1. In bottom of soup pot, sauté the chopped onions and garlic in the butter.
2. Add the water, spices, and lentils. Bring to a boil.
3. With the children's help, chop all the vegetables.
4. Add the vegetables that take longer to cook first (such as potato, carrot, and celery).
5. Continue cooking soup and adding vegetables as the children finish chopping them.
6. Simmer for 1 hour, adding noodles near the end, if desired.

Shared by Heather Cohill ~
Waldorf School of Baltimore, Maryland

Merriconeag School Soup

water
3/4 cup brown rice
3 or 4 large carrots
1 T. Italian herbs (or herbs from the children's garden)
1 cup pasta or small noodles (or more if the children are really hungry)
1 heaping T. Plantiforce bouillon
vegetables brought by the children

1. Chop all the vegetables with the children.
2. Fill a large pot 1/2 way up with water.
3. Add all ingredients to the pot and simmer until tender.

Shared by Bridget Jeffers ~
Merriconeag Waldorf School, Maine

My Recipes

5. Luscious Fruits

This is a very short chapter, for fruit is not included very often in a "recipe" form on the snack menus that I collected. Only two recipes, one for apple/pear sauce and one for apple crisp appear on the next page.

However, fruit does seem to make a more frequent appearance in its simplest state — raw. Several schools include a fruit salad as part of their snack. Others offer apples slices as part of the snack.

Raisins also seem to be a common "extra" offered to the children as part of their snack. Raisins help make the snack extra festive when they are added to porridges or breads.

A Story to Share

One teacher told me they add raisins to *everything* during Advent. Raisins in the porridge, bread... sounds yummy. But do they really put raisins in the vegetable soup?! Hmm... I wonder?

Apple/Pear Sauce

Pockets bulge with apples on Thursdays at the Great Barrington Rudolf Steiner School. Sometimes I even see an apple or two bouncing across the parking lot. It's a good thing they get used for applesauce!
~Lisa Hildreth

Served with Millet Squares (see the "A Grain a Day" chapter for the recipe) or over oatmeal.

apples
pears
water

1. Add an inch of water to the bottom of a large pot and bring to a boil.
2. With the children's help, cut apples and pears into small chunks.
3. Add chopped fruit to pot and simmer until tender and most of the water has evaporated.
4. Allow sauce to cool a bit and then run it though the food mill to remove any peels and seeds.

Shared by Diane Prusha ~
Great Barrington Rudolf Steiner School,
Massachusetts

Apple Crisp

This dish is a big favorite at Andy's Parent/ Toddler classes at the Hawthorne Valley school. When I visited her class, I watched the 2- and 3- year-old children proudly put their apples on the peeler/slicer/corer machine and turn the crank. They were amazingly adept at this job and enjoyed nibbling on the peels and any other little tidbits they could find.
~Lisa Hildreth

lots of apples, peeled and sliced
cinnamon
maple syrup

Topping:
    4-5 cups oats
    1 stick of butter, melted
    1/2 cup maple syrup
    2 T. oil
    pinch of salt

1. Parents help the children use the peeler/ slicer/corer machine to prepare the apples they brought from home.
2. Preheat oven to 350°.
3. Place apples in a 9 x 13-inch baking pan.
4. Sprinkle the apples with cinnamon and a few tablespoons of maple syrup.
5. Mix together the topping ingredients and sprinkle over the apples.
6. Bake for 45 minutes to 1 hour.

Shared by Andy Ward ~
Hawthorne Valley Waldorf School,
New York

6. A Grain a Day

We can give the children in our classes a precious gift by introducing them to whole grains, especially in a simple cooked form. At a conference, I met a teacher who said that she grinds, cooks, and serves the grain of the day as the morning snack. She even served us a simple rye porridge with tamari. It was delicious and I was intrigued. When I tried to ask her for the "recipe" she was surprised and said it was just cooked rye. (But I never cooked or ate such a thing in my whole life!)

This chapter provides you with some thoughts about grains and a variety of recipes containing grains.

A Different Grain for Each Day

In the Waldorf kindergarten we, as teachers, are conscious of and celebrate many types of cosmic rhythms: day and night, the seasons, the days of the week. As part of this recognition of cosmic rhythms, quite a few teachers told me that they cook grains according to the rhythm of the days of the week.

Emma Graf in her book, *Cooking with Grains*, reminds us of the cosmic origins of the days of the week — for the Sun, Moon, Mars, Mercury, Jupiter, Venus, and Saturn are the 7 heavenly bodies that give us the names of the days of the week (although the origin of the names of the weekdays are often more obvious in languages other than English) (pg. 2). The grains reflect the cosmic forces rayed down from these heavenly bodies and are therefore associated with different days as follows (pg. 3):

Sunday	Sun	Wheat
Monday	Moon	Rice
Tuesday	Mars	Barley
Wednesday	Mercury	Millet
Thursday	Jupiter	Rye
Friday	Venus	Oats
Saturday	Saturn	Maize (Corn)

How Do these Grains Affect Human Beings?

In *Cooking with Grains*, Emma Graf also explains how these different grains affect us:

• *Wheat* —helps to harmonize the organ systems. It also "supports the processes in the sense-nerve system and the metabolism and so relaxes the rhythmical middle" (pg. 18). Wheat is grown world-wide (pg. 17).

• *Rice* — acts more on the digestive system than the nerve-sense system and therefore does not stimulate a wakeful consciousness (pg. 34). Rice is one of the main foods of the peoples of India and the Far East (pg. 33).

• *Barley* — the "dual effect of barley, related to the silica and sugar contents, is seen in two areas of the human organism: the nervous system and the connective tissue, as well as the metabolism and muscles" (pg. 41). Its silica content can strengthen ligaments and tissues and its sugar content can aid in soothing irritations of the mucous membranes of the stomach and intestines (pgs. 41-42). Barley was a staple food of the Greeks (pg. 41).

• *Millet* — stimulates the warmth processes. It also is good for skin, hair, eyes, and teeth. Millet has a low calcium content and should be balanced with the addition of milk (pgs. 49-50). Millet is grown in Africa, America, India, and Russia (pg. 49).

• *Rye* — "stimulates the formative forces in the human being and gives strength for uprightness. The carbohydrates of rye are strongly influenced by the light. Form, breathing and speech are connected with the metabolism of carbohydrates. Rye nourishes head and bones but also heart and lung are strengthened through the formative forces" (pg. 58). The strong Celtic and Slovenian folk tribes ate rye as their predominant grain (pg. 57).

• *Oats* — "have a positive stimulatory effect on the digestive and metabolic system, which is also the centre of the will. We find in oats a particularly strengthening element which helps in loosening stiffness. With depression and lack of motivation it activates and improves the frame of mind. Increased stamina, reduced tiredness, improved resistance to disease, are qualities... attributed to oats" (pg. 66). It is believed that oats were first cultivated in Europe, and oats have been connected to the German people (pg. 65).

• *Maize (Corn)* — the protein in maize does not contain gluten, which is helpful for those suffering from gluten allergies. Maize also helps stimulate the metabolism in muscles (pg. 74). Maize was a staple food in the diet of the Native Americans (pg. 73).

Soaking and Fermenting Grains

In *Nourishing Traditions*, Sally Fallon notes that virtually all ancient peoples soaked or fermented their grains before eating them in breads, porridges, or cakes. This ancient wisdom has been confirmed by modern science by the discovery of phytic acid in the outer layer of all grains. In the intestine, phytic acid combines with calcium, magnesium, copper, iron, and zinc and blocks the absorption of these essential minerals. Therefore, a diet high in untreated whole grains can lead to mineral deficiencies and bone loss. However, soaking grains overnight allows enzymes, lactobacilli, and other organisms to neutralize the phytic acid (pg. 452).

Similarly, science has found that many people have trouble digesting some of the proteins (especially gluten) in grains. This problem is also alleviated by the soaking and fermenting process, which helps break down these proteins into components that can be easily absorbed (pg. 453).

Therefore, Ms. Fallon recommends that all grains containing gluten, such as wheat, oats, rye, and barley should be soaked or fermented. Whole rice and millet, which do not contain gluten, and also have lower amounts of phytic acid, do not have to be soaked. Instead, she suggests steaming them for at least 2 hours. Ground rice and millet may be cooked without preparation (pg. 453).

Incorporating Grains in Your Snacks

Most teachers I spoke to included at least 3 different grains in their weekly menus. Some examples of these grains and how they are incorporated into the snacks appear below:

Wheat	bread, pretzels
Rice	cooked rice, rice porridge, rice cakes, rice pudding
Barley	cooked barley, barley in soup, barley in a stir fry
Millet	cooked millet, millet cakes
Rye	cooked rye, rye crackers, rye bread
Oats	oatmeal, oatbars, oat flakes or rolled oats in bread, oats as topping on apple crisp, oats in granola
Corn	popcorn, cornbread, tortilla chips

Granola

The children enjoy helping to crush the almonds for this snack. They use wooden spoons on a wooden board to do the job.

Serve with vanilla rice dream. Feeds 16 children (and 2 teachers).

rolled oats
2 apples, peeled and grated
2 T. maple syrup
2 T. oil or butter
1/4 to 1/2 cup crushed whole almonds
shredded coconut (optional)
raisins (optional)

1. Preheat oven to 350°.
2. Fill two 1-pound loaf pans 3/4 full of rolled oats.
3. In a bowl, mix the grated apples, maple syrup, and oil (or butter) into a moist paste.
4. Mix everything in the 2 loaf pans, *except* the raisins (optional).
5. Put pans in the oven and bake for about 30 minutes, stirring it whenever the top is brown.
6. If you are putting raisins in your granola, add them now, after it is finished baking.

Shared by Milicent Pittis ~
Housatonic Valley Waldorf School,
Connecticut

Rice Porridge

Served with maple syrup.

ground rice
water

1. Grind rice with children. You may wish to do the grinding in advance.
2. Pour rice and water into a large pot in the ratio of about 1 part rice to 4 parts water. (For example, add 2 cups of rice and 8 cups of water to the pot.)
3. Turn heat to high and stir constantly with a wire whisk until rice is dissolved in hot water.
4. Reduce heat to low and stir occasionally until the desired thickness.

Shared by Diane Prusha ~
Great Barrington Rudolf Steiner School,
Massachusetts

Millet Cakes

Served with jam.

3 cups millet
6 cups water
1-1/2 cups flour
3 t. salt
ground ginger (optional)
oil (preferably walnut or safflower oil)

1. Put millet and water into a pot and bring to a boil.
2. Reduce heat, cover, and simmer for about 20 minutes or until all the water is absorbed. Do *not* stir the pot.
3. In a bowl, mix the cooked millet with the flour, salt, (and ginger, if desired).

4. Form into patties, brush each with oil, and place on a cookie sheet.
5. Bake at 375° for 10 minutes on each side.

Shared by Brooke Redgrave ~
The Pine Tree Room, a Waldorf home care
program in Baltimore, Maryland

Oatbars

Heather found that some of the children were arriving at the Dandelion Room really hungry in the morning. To meet this need and fill those tummies, the teachers began making oatbars as a "breakfast" snack. A plate of oatbars is set out in the morning until all the children have arrived.

4 cups muesli
5 T. canola oil
2 T. honey
1 t. cinnamon
1 t. vanilla
1 egg, beaten

1. Preheat oven to 325° and grease a shallow 7 x 11-inch baking dish.
2. In a large bowl, mix all ingredients together.
3. Spoon into the pan, patting the mixture until it is level.
4. Bake for 30 to 35 minutes, or until light brown around the edges. Cool for a couple of minutes and then mark it into 12 to 16 bars.
5. When completely cool, break bars as marked.

Shared by Heather Cohill ~
Waldorf School of Baltimore, Maryland

Millet Squares

*When some of the teachers at the Great
Barrington Rudolf Steiner School heard about
the warming properties of millet, they decided to
give it a try. They replaced their oatmeal porridge with millet porridge, but many of the
children would not eat it. Then a parent who was
experienced in macrobiotic cooking gave them a
new recipe to try. It was a winner!*

*Served with apple/pear sauce. See the "Luscious
Fruits" chapter for this recipe.*

3 cups millet
6 cups water
1/4 or 1/3 cup maple syrup

1. Over medium heat, toast millet in bottom
   of a large pot until you start to smell the
   millet (optional).
2. Add water and syrup to the pot and
   bring to a boil.
3. Reduce heat, cover, and cook at a slow
   boil for about 20 minutes. Do *not* stir the
   pot.
4. When all the water is absorbed, pour
   millet into a glass 9 x 13-inch baking dish
   and allow to cool and harden.
5. Cut into small squares.

*Shared by Diane Prusha ~
Great Barrington Rudolf Steiner School,
Massachusetts*

Rice Pudding

*This pudding is one of the children's favorite
snacks at the Mossy Rock Children's Garden, a
home care in Connecticut. Susan says the pot is
scraped clean at every serving! Recipe **feeds 6**
children; multiply it as necessary.*

1 cup cooked rice (basmati works well)
1/4 t. salt
1 egg, beaten (collected from the chickens)
3 T. honey
currents, raisins, or chopped almonds
milk or cream
1 or 2 drops of rosewater

1. Mix rice, salt, egg, honey, and currents,
   raisins, or almonds in a large pot.
2. Pour the milk or cream into the pot until
   it is level with the top of the rice.
3. Cook over low heat for 5 to 8 minutes.
4. Add the drop of rosewater just before
   serving (more is overpowering).

*Shared by Susan Lynch ~
Mossy Rock Children's Garden,
Danielson, Connecticut*

Oatmeal Porridge

Served with maple syrup.

oatmeal
water
pinch of salt
cinnamon

1. Pour oatmeal and water into a large pot in the ratio of about 1 part oatmeal to 2 parts water. (For example, add 6 cups of oatmeal and 12 cups of water to the pot.)
2. Add the salt and cinnamon.
3. Turn heat to high and stir occasionally until boiling.
4. Reduce heat and stir occasionally until the desired thickness.

Shared by Jill Farrell ~
Green Meadow Waldorf School, New York

Popcorn

popping corn
olive oil
salt

1. Pour 1/8 inch of olive oil into the bottom of a large pot and heat on high until very hot.
2. Add 3 kernels to test the oil.
3. When test kernels pop, cover the bottom of the pan with popping corn.
4. Quickly cover pot and shake pot rapidly back and forth over high heat.
5. When pot is full and popping ceases, remove it from the heat and set aside.
6. Pour into bowl and sprinkle with salt.

Shared by Diane Prusha ~
Great Barrington Rudolf Steiner School, Massachusetts

Rice Pilaf

An easy snack that takes care of itself.

2-1/2 cups brown rice
1/2 cup mixed grains (mix of rye berries, millet, and barley)
6 cups water
Braggs Liquid Aminos

1. Pour rice, mixed grains, and water into a rice cooker.
2. Cook according to the directions for your rice cooker.
3. Sprinkle with Braggs Liquid Aminos before serving.

Shared by Ruth Kasl ~
Susquehanna Waldorf School, Pennsylvania

Pretzels

1-1/2 cups warm water
1 t. yeast
4 t. honey
salt
about 3 cups whole wheat flour
about 3 cups white flour

1. In a large bowl, mix the water, yeast, and honey, and wait until the yeast foams.
2. Preheat oven to 425°.
3. Stir in salt and flour, gradually adding flour until the dough is elastic.
4. Shape and bake on a greased cookie sheet for 10-12 minutes (turning once).

Shared by Heather Cohill ~
Waldorf School of Baltimore, Maryland

Oatmeal-Carrot Muffins

1 cup oats
2 cups whole wheat pastry flour
2 t. baking powder
1/4 t. salt
1 egg, lightly beaten
1/2 cup maple syrup
1 cup milk
1/4 cup vegetable oil
2 grated carrots
1 cup raisins
1 chopped pear (optional)

1. Preheat oven to 400°.
2. In a large bowl, combine oats, flour, baking powder, and salt.
3. In a small bowl, beat the egg and then add the maple syrup, milk, oil, and grated carrots. Mix well.
4. Pour the wet ingredients into the large bowl with the dry ingredients. Stir until just blended.
5. Stir in the raisins and chopped pear (optional).
6. Divide batter into 12 muffin cups and bake for 20 to 25 minutes.

Shared by Lisa Hildreth ~
Susquehanna Waldorf School, Pennsylvania

Apple Cookies

I got this recipe by following my nose — right into the parent/child classroom at my school one day! Jackie told me that this was a new favorite snack and offered me a cookie.
  ~ Lisa Hildreth

Wet Ingredients:
  2 cups rolled oats
  1 can frozen apple juice concentrate
  1 large spoonful tahini
  1 very ripe banana, mashed
  1/3 cups honey

Dry Ingredients:
  2 cups whole wheat flour or corn flour
  a sprinkle of raisins
  a sprinkle of walnuts
  cinnamon to taste
  a sprinkle of salt
  1 t. baking powder

1. Combine all the wet ingredients and let sit until the oats absorb the moisture.
2. Preheat oven to 350°.
3. Mix the dry ingredients together and stir into the wet mixture.
4. Shape into cookies and bake on cookie sheet for 15 to 20 minutes.

Shared by Jackie Randazzo ~
Susquehanna Waldorf School, Pennsylvania

Basic Grains - Pilaf Style

Offered to help you begin to experiment with cooking the 7 grains.

1 cup grain
2 to 3 cups water

1. Consider soaking the grain overnight. (See the "Soaking and Fermenting Grains" section earlier in this chapter.)
2. Place grain and water in a pot and heat on high until boiling. *Do not stir* the grain at any time during the cooking process!
3. Turn heat down to low, cover, and simmer until all the water is absorbed.
4. Fluff grain with a fork.

Shared by Lisa Hildreth ~
Susquehanna Waldorf School, Pennsylvania

Basic Grain Porridge

Offered to help you begin to experiment with cooking the 7 grains.

1 cup grain
3 to 4 cups water

1. Consider grinding the grain with the children's help.
2. Consider soaking the grain overnight. (See the "Soaking and Fermenting Grains" section earlier in this chapter.)
3. Place grain and water in a pot and heat on high until boiling.
4. Turn heat down to low, cover, and simmer slowly until porridge is the desired thickness.
5. Stir occasionally. Add more water if porridge becomes too thick.

Shared by Lisa Hildreth ~
Susquehanna Waldorf School, Pennsylvania

7. Happy Birthday Cakes and Muffins

Birthdays are one of the special festivals in the Waldorf kindergarten and are a time to celebrate the individual child and his or her family. Food plays an important part in this celebration and every teacher I spoke to has some kind of special cake or food to serve on birthdays.

This chapter provides some thoughts to consider when you are planning your birthday menu. It also provides numerous recipes for tried-and-true birthday cakes and muffins.

Some Thoughts to Consider

• *Who will make the special birthday snack?* What part will the children play in preparing the birthday feast? Will they bake the cake or will the parents? Will there be any additional food to go with the cake, and who will make it?

• *If the parents bake something for the birthday, will you supply the recipe?* Some teachers have found it easier to give all the parents one special birthday recipe. This way you know what you are getting, and the children know what to expect. Other teachers prefer to provide the parents with guidelines, and then leave them free to choose the recipe. For example, you might ask them to bake using maple syrup rather than sugar.

• *Will the birthday snack replace the snack of the day or be additional food?* Some teachers serve their regular snack and then add the birthday cake as desert. Others replace the snack of the day with a special birthday snack or the cake.

• *Will you use sugar in your birthday cake or muffin?* Some recipes in this chapter include sugar, but most use maple syrup, honey, or molasses. If you are avoiding refined sugar, but still wish to try one of the "sugar" recipes, I suggest substituting maple syrup. I have used maple syrup as my favorite baking sweetener for many years, and have found that it has a more subtle flavor than honey. You will need less maple syrup than the amount of sugar the recipe calls for (for example, if the recipe requires 1 cup of sugar, use 1/2 or 2/3 cup of maple syrup instead). Please refer to the "What about Sugar?" section of chapter 1 for more information about different kinds of sweetners.

Some Stories to Share

At the Rudolf Steiner School in New York City, the children make a birthday cake in class and the parents bring in fruit, cheese, and crackers.

In my sons' classes at Green Meadow Waldorf School, the parents baked the birthday muffins and the children whipped cream and sliced strawberries to go with the muffins. In the Nursery class at this same school (where I used to teach), we ate our daily snack as usual. Then we enjoyed our birthday muffins at the end of the morning in our birthday circle.

At the Great Barrington Rudolf Steiner School, the assistant teachers make popcorn to serve with the cake or muffins brought in by the parents. All is eaten at the regular snack time.

In Lise Stoessel's Nursery class at the Charlottesville Waldorf School, the parents bake the cake, using her whole-grain recipe. Lise dusts the cake with confectioners' sugar and serves it with apple wedges, raisins, and juicy tea. (The recipe for juicy tea appears in the "Festival Foods" chapter.)

At the Green Mountain Waldorf School, the children in Nancy Segretto's class enjoyed a birthday cake they made in class. The birthday child's parents brought the whipped cream.

Honey Cake

This cake is delicious plain or with just a sprinkle of powdered sugar. Some teachers at the Garden City school add "wishing raisins" to their cakes — each child adds a raisin to the batter and makes a wish in his or her heart for the birthday child.

1 cup butter
1-1/2 cups honey
4 large eggs
1 cup milk
3 cups unbleached flour (or combination of white and whole wheat flours)
1 T. double acting baking powder
1/8 t. salt

1. Preheat oven to 350°.
2. Butter and flour the baking pans. You may use either a 10-inch tube pan or two 9-inch cake pans.
3. Cream butter and honey.
4. Beat in eggs, one at a time.
5. Sift the flour with the baking powder and salt. Then add it to the creamed butter mixture, alternating between adding flour and milk.
6. Beat for at least 3 minutes or until well blended.
7. Pour into the buttered and floured pan(s).
8. Bake for about 1 hour if using a tube pan or 35 minutes if using the cake pans. Test with a cake tester or toothpick.
9. Let cool for about 30 minutes for the tube pan or about 10 to 15 minutes for the cake pans before turning out on a rack to finish cooling.

Shared by Patricia Foster ~
Waldorf School of Garden City, New York

Applesauce Birthday Cake

To make their birthday cake extra festive, the teachers at the Merriconeag Waldorf School like to bake this cake in a bundt pan, sprinkle the top with powdered sugar, and place a vase with seasonal flowers in the middle.

1 stick of butter
1 cup honey
2 cups chunk-style applesauce
1 t. vanilla
3 cups unbleached flour
1 t. cinnamon
1/2 t. nutmeg
2 t. baking soda

1. Preheat oven to 325°.
2. Butter and flour a 10-inch tube pan or bundt pan.
3. Cream together butter and honey.
4. Stir in applesauce and vanilla, mixing thoroughly.
5. Sift flour, cinnamon, nutmeg, and baking soda over the applesauce mixture. Stir well.
6. Pour batter into pan and set on the middle rack of oven. Bake for 70 to 75 minutes or until cake tester comes out clean.
7. Cool in pan for 15 minutes. Turn onto a rack to cool.

Shared by Bridget Jeffers ~
Merriconeag Waldorf School, Maine

Carob Spice Cake

A great cake with no eggs or dairy!

Wet Ingredients:
    2 T. vinegar
    2 t. vanilla
    1-3/4 cups cold water
    1-1/2 cups maple syrup

Dry Ingredients:
    2 cups whole wheat flour
    1 cup unbleached white flour
    1 t. salt
    1/2 cup carob powder
    3 t. baking soda
    2 t. cinnamon

1. Preheat oven to 350°.
2. Mix the wet ingredients in a large bowl and set aside.
3. Mix the dry ingredients.
4. Add the dry ingredients to the wet ingredients and mix well.
5. Pour batter into a well buttered/oiled bundt pan and bake for 50 minutes.

Shared by Lilian Chiu ~
Acorn Hill, Maryland

Birthday Cake in a Pan

You can use an 8-inch spring-form pan and mix the ingredients right in the pan. Each child may be given a handful of "wishing" berries or raisins and add them to the cake while making a wish for the birthday child. When the cake has cooled, the birthday child may sprinkle powdered sugar on top.

1-1/2 cups whole wheat pastry flour
1/3 cup carob powder
1 t. baking soda
1/2 t. salt
1/3 cup honey
1 t. vanilla
1 t. vinegar
1/3 cup oil
1 to 1-1/4 cups of water

1. Preheat oven to 350°.
2. Combine the dry ingredients in an ungreased pan.
3. Add the honey, vanilla, vinegar, oil, and water.
4. Blend with fork, scraping sides to be sure all flour is mixed in. Batter should be of cake consistency, or perhaps a bit thicker.
5. Bake 25 to 30 minutes.

*Shared by Connie Manson ~
Sunbridge College, New York*

Yogurt Birthday Cake

Wet Ingredients:
    1 cup vegetable oil
    1 cup honey
    1 2/3 cups of vanilla yogurt
    2 t. vanilla

Dry Ingredients:
    4 cups pastry flour
    1 t. baking soda
    3/4 t. salt

1. Preheat oven to 350°.
2. Mix the wet ingredients in a large bowl and set aside.
3. Mix the dry ingredients.
4. Add the dry ingredients to the wet ingredients and mix well.
5. Pour into a greased and floured 9 x 13-inch pan and bake for about 40 minutes.

*Shared by Heather Cohill ~
Waldorf School of Baltimore, Maryland*

Tofu Pudding Cake

No dairy! Carolyn uses Mori-Nu Mates vanilla lowfat pudding mix and Mori-Nu Lite Silken Tofu when she bakes this cake.

1 package tofu pudding mix
1 container silken tofu
1-1/2 sticks of margarine
1 cup sugar
1 t. vanilla
2-1/2 cups unbleached white flour
1/2 t. baking soda
1 t. baking powder
1/2 t. salt

1. Preheat oven to 350°.
2. Grease a 9-inch round cake pan.
3. With an electric mixer, beat together the tofu and pudding mix until fluffy.
4. In a large bowl, cream the margarine, sugar, and vanilla.
5. Mix the dry ingredients together in a separate bowl.
6. Add the flour and pudding mixtures alternately to the creamed margarine and sugar. Combine well. (Batter is doughy.)
7. Pour into prepared pan and bake for 35 to 45 minutes.

*Shared by Carolyn Lin ~
Rudolf Steiner School, New York*

Nursery Birthday Cake

This recipe makes two layers. Bring one to the class party and save one for yourself at home! Or use the recipe to make muffins.

3-1/2 cups whole wheat flour
1 cup sugar
4 t. baking powder
2 t. salt
2+ t. cinnamon
1 stick of butter (softened)
1 cup milk
4 eggs
1 t. vanilla
1/2 cup honey
1/2 cup milk + 1/2 cup water

1. Preheat oven to 350°.
2. Butter two 9-inch round cake pans.
3. Mix dry ingredients.
4. Add softened butter to dry ingredients and mix with your fingers to ensure uniform distribution.
5. In a separate bowl, mix the milk, eggs, vanilla, and honey.
6. Add wet ingredients to the dry and mix until a creamy batter has formed (adding some or all of the milk and water mixture, as necessary).
7. Pour into the buttered pans and bake for 20 to 25 minutes.
8. When cool, dust with maple sugar powder or confectioner's sugar.

Shared by Lise Stoessel ~
Charlottesville Waldorf School, Virginia

Maple Cake

1/2 cup butter
1/2 cup sugar
2 eggs, lightly beaten
3/4 cup maple syrup
1/2 cup milk
2-1/2 cups cake flour
2-1/2 t. baking powder
2/3 t. (scant) soda
1/2 t. ginger (optional)

1. Preheat oven to 350°.
2. Cream the butter and sugar.
3. Add the beaten eggs and syrup.
4. Sift the flour, baking powder, soda, and ginger (if desired).
5. Add the sifted dry ingredients to the bowl, alternating with milk. Mix well.
6. Bake in tube pan for about 50 minutes or in 9-inch cake pans for about 35 minutes.

Shared by Patricia Foster ~
Waldorf School of Garden City, New York

Carrot Cake

No eggs or dairy! The children at the Rudolf Steiner School in New York City enjoy this cake every Friday. I chose to include the recipe in the birthday chapter.
~ Lisa Hildreth

Served with cream cheese.

Dry Ingredients:
2 cups pastry flour
1/2 cup unbleached white flour
1/2 t. sea salt
2 T. baking powder
1 T. cinnamon
1/4 t. nutmeg
1/4 t. cloves
1 cup walnuts
1 cup raisins

Wet Ingredients:
1/2 cup corn oil
1 cup maple syrup
1/2 cup soymilk
1 cup apple juice
1 t. vanilla
1/3 cup grated carrot

1. Preheat oven to 325 or 350°.
2. In a large bowl, combine all the dry ingredients and mix well with a whisk. Set aside.
3. In a separate bowl, combine all the wet ingredients (except carrot) and mix well with a whisk.
4. Pour the wet mixture into the dry mixture. Using a whisk, combine them until only just mixed. Do not overmix.
5. Add the carrot to the mixture, stirring gently.

6. Pour batter into a 9 x 13-inch glass baking dish and bake for 50 minutes.
7. Let cool on a wire rack.

Shared by Carolyn Lin ~
Rudolf Steiner School, New York

Honey Muffins

No eggs or dairy! Monday is muffin day at the Rudolf Steiner School in New York City. These muffins could also be used for birthdays.

2-1/2 cups flour
1/2 cup honey
2 t. vanilla
1 cup soymilk, almond milk, or rice dream
1/4 cup oil
2 t. baking powder
pinch of salt

1. Preheat oven to 350°.
2. Oil and flour the muffin pans.
3. In large bowl, mix all ingredients until just blended.
4. Bake for 30 minutes.

Shared by Carolyn Lin ~
Rudolf Steiner School, New York

Blueberry Muffins

Dry Ingredients:
   3 cups unbleached white flour
   1 cup whole wheat pastry flour
   1/2 t. sea salt
   2 T. baking powder

Wet Ingredients:
   1/2 cup corn oil
   1/2 cup maple syrup
   1/2 rice syrup
   1/2 cup soymilk
   1-1/2 cups apple juice
   1 T. vanilla

1/2 pint blueberries

1. Preheat oven to 325°.
2. Oil the muffin pans with corn oil or set paper muffin cups in the pan.
3. In a large bowl, combine all the dry ingredients and mix well with a whisk. Set aside.
4. In a separate bowl, combine all the wet ingredients and mix well with a whisk.
5. Pour the wet mixture into the dry mixture. Using a whisk, stir them until just mixed. Do not overmix.
6. Add the blueberries, stirring gently with a rubber spatula.
7. Fill the muffin cups and bake for 50 minutes to 1 hour, or until the edges of the muffins are golden brown.

Shared by Diane Prusha ~
Great Barrington Rudolf Steiner School, Massachusetts

Birthday Star Cookies

1/4 cup oil
1/2 cup honey
1/4 cup molasses
2-1/2 cups flour (mix of whole wheat and unbleached white)
1 t. baking soda
2 t. cinnamon
1 t. ginger
1/2 t. salt

1. Preheat oven to 350°.
2. In large bowl, combine oil, honey, and molasses.
3. Sift the remaining ingredients and add to wet mixture, stirring until blended.
4. Roll out dough on a floured surface.
5. Use cookie cutter to cut out stars.
6. Bake for 5 to 9 minutes, depending on thickness.

Shared by Ruth Kasl ~
Susquehanna Waldorf School, Pennsylvania

Pumpkin Muffins

Dry Ingredients:
    2 cups unbleached white flour
    1-1/2 cups whole wheat pastry flour
    1/2 t. sea salt
    2 T. baking powder

Wet Ingredients:
    1/2 cup corn oil
    1 cup maple syrup
    1/2 cup soymilk
    1 cup apple juice
    1 cup pumpkin or butternut squash,
    (cooked)

1. Cut pumpkin or squash and dice into medium-sized pieces. Cook in a small amount of water.
2. Using a food processor, purée the pumpkin or squash (make sure it's not too wet). Set aside.
3. Preheat oven to 325°.
4. Oil the muffin pans with corn oil or set paper muffin cups in the pan.
5. In a large bowl, combine all the dry ingredients and mix well with a whisk. Set aside.
6. In a separate bowl, combine all the wet ingredients and mix well with a whisk.
7. Pour the wet mixture into the dry mixture. Using a whisk, stir them until just mixed. Do not overmix.
8. Fill the muffin cups and bake for 50 minutes to 1 hour, or until the edges of the muffins are golden brown.

Shared by Diane Prusha ~
Great Barrington Rudolf Steiner School,
Massachusetts

8. Festival Foods

How will you celebrate a festival in your classroom and what part will food play in that celebration? It can range from an elaborate feast, requiring many days of preparation, to something as simple as adding raisins and walnuts to your regular bread recipe.

For example, Annamay Keeney, from the Waldorf School of Atlanta shared, "I bring in or we make perhaps one extra thing to go with or enhance our regular snack." And she gave some examples:

- noodles in the soup
- a special spread for crackers
- applesauce at harvest time
- cornbread
- honey butter
- sprinkling raisins and cinnamon on buns
- forming their bread dough into a wheat sheaf
- fresh strawberries in spring

This chapter provides some thoughts to consider when you are planning your festival foods, examples of what other teachers serve for the festivals, and some recipes.

Some Thoughts to Consider

• *How does the food for a festival support that festival?* Of course, certain foods are traditionally associated with seasons (such as pumpkins with Halloween), but you can also reflect the festival by including images or symbols from the festival as part of the food. For example, consider dragon-shaped

bread for Michaelmas, star cookies at advent, or hot cross buns for Easter. Sometimes teachers serve food that appears in the story that they tell for the festival.

• *Who will prepare the food?* Will the children prepare all the food, working in advance if necessary? Or will you ask parents to make some of the festival foods? Some teachers prepare the festival treat at home the night before.

• *What other activities can you do with the children that are related to the food preparation?* For example, one teacher I spoke to takes the class to the orchard to pick apples and then makes applebutter with the children. The applebutter is then saved for their Michaelmas celebration. Another teacher shared that they husk the corn, grind it, and then make cornbread. They also save the husks to make cornhusk dolls.

Examples of Festival Foods

The following are some of the foods that the different teachers I spoke to make for the festivals. *If an item is marked with an asterisk (*), the recipe is included in this chapter.*

Michaelmas
- dragon bread,* fresh butter, cider
- apple cake*
- harvest bread in wheat sheaf form* and purple concord grapes
- bread with applebutter

Halloween
- pumpkin muffins, pumpkin seeds, sliced apples, cider

Lantern Walk
- stone soup and baked apples
- popcorn and hot cider
- Rose Room oatmeal cookies*

Martinmas
- soup

Thanksgiving or Harvest Festival
- pumpkin pie
- pumpkin cake, pumpkin seeds, harvest bread in wheat sheaf form*
- large loaf of bread and grapes
- applesauce, cornbread and honey butter
- grind corn with children and make cornbread with butter

St. Nicholas
- gingerbread cookies
- honey cake,* nuts, apples
- star cookies, oranges, nuts (see birthday chapter for cookie recipe)

Advent (or Advent Spiral)
- star cookies
- add walnuts and raisins to bread, add raisins to porridge and applesauce
- thumbprint oatmeal cookies*

Santa Lucia
- Santa Lucia buns*

Christmas or Winter Holidays
- gingerbread
- gingerbread men and women*
- cookie cutter cookies

Valentine's Day
- oatmeal heart cookies with raspberry jam
- Valentine tarts*
- Valentine cookies*
- heart cookies and strawberries

Saint Patrick's Day
- Irish soda bread*

Passover
- matzo with apple walnut chutney or butter
- seder platter

Easter
- challah bread (with eggs)
- carrot cake
- bread bunnies, hard boiled eggs
- hot cross buns
- braided loaf with hard boiled eggs baked in loaf
- cardamom bread

Dragon Bread

For Michaelmas. This loaf is a special shape rather than a special recipe. The teachers who make this loaf use their regular bread recipe and then shape the dough as described below.

1. Create the dragon's head, body, and tail.
2. Use more dough to create lots of spikes!

Shared by Nancy Segreto ~
Green Mountain Waldorf School, Vermont

---

1. Create the dragon's head, body, and tail.
2. Add almonds for the scales.
3. Use a raisin for the eye and red fruit for fire.

Shared by Maryla Sikora ~
Four Winds School, Illinois

Apple Cake

The fairies leave this cake in the woods on the Festival of Courage (Michaelmas). At The Pine Tree Room, one teacher places herself in the woods dressed as a very woodsy Mother Earth character. She waits, playing her instrument, surrounded with the bounty of autumn (pumpkins, gourds, mums, a basket of apples, and some bulbs). The other teacher takes the children for a walk. They hear the music and follow it until they find "Mother Earth." She tells them a story about courage and gives them each an apple and a bulb. Then the children continue on their way until they see some petals scattered on the ground. It leads them to this apple cake. Perhaps the woodland fairies left it for them?

2-1/2 cups grated apple
2 cups raisins
1-1/2 cups boiling water
3 T. oil
1 cup + 2 T. maple syrup
1-1/2 t. cinnamon
1-1/2 t. allspice
1/2 t. cloves
1-1/2 t. salt
1-1/2 cups whole wheat pastry flour
1-1/2 cups white flour
1-1/2 t. baking soda
3/4 cup chopped walnuts

1. Pour boiling water over the apples and raisins. Pour oil on top and let stand 10 minutes.
2. Add the maple syrup and spices (including salt). Allow to cool.
3. Preheat the oven to 350°.
4. Sift together the flour, baking soda, and add the walnuts. Combine with other ingredients.
5. Pour batter into a well-greased tube pan, or two loaf pans.
6. Bake for 45 minutes to 1 hour.

Shared by Brooke Redgrave ~ The Pine Tree Room, a Waldorf home care in Baltimore, Maryland

---

Harvest Wheat-Sheaf Bread

This loaf is a special shape rather than a special recipe. The teachers who make this loaf use their regular bread recipe and then shape the dough as described below. For harvest festival or Thanksgiving.

Served on a huge bread board with butter and grapes.

1. Children roll all the dough into long, thin, "snakes."
2. Have a few children roll out an extra long piece of dough.
3. Arrange all the shorter "snakes" on a cookie sheet to be the wheat.
4. Use the longest "snake" to wrap around the "wheat" and tie it into a bow.
5. Snip the ends of the "snakes" to make it look like a sheaf of wheat.
6. Bake at 350° for about 30 minutes or until done.

Shared by Diane Prusha ~
Great Barrington Rudolf Steiner School, Massachusetts

Served with pumpkin cake and pumpkin seeds.

1. Follow steps above to form the basic wheat sheaf form.
2. Add oats to be the grains at the top.
3. Make a little dough mouse and place him at the bottom where he can nibble the sheaf!

Shared by Lise Stoessel ~
Charlottesville Waldorf School, Virginia

Honey Cake 1

Contains no eggs or dairy! Saint Nicholas leaves this delicious cake, along with nuts and apples at the doors of the kindergartens at the Great Barrington Rudolf Steiner School.

1/4 cup soy margarine (or butter)
1/2 cup honey
1 t. vanilla
1/4 t. salt
2 cups whole wheat flour
1 t. baking soda
1 t. cinnamon
1 t. cream of tartar
2/3 cup water or soymilk (or other milk)

1. Preheat the oven to 325°.
2. Beat margarine, honey, vanilla, and salt together.
3. Combine flour, soda, cinnamon, and cream of tartar.
4. Stir dry ingredients into beaten mixture alternately with hot water or milk.
5. Pour into well-oiled 9-inch square baking pan and bake for 30 minutes or until done.

Shared by Christine Inglis ~
Great Barrington Rudolf Steiner School, Massachusetts

Honey Cake 2

For Saint Nicholas day.

1/2 cup butter
1 cup honey
2 eggs
3/4 cup buttermilk
2-1/2 cups flour
1 t. baking soda
1 t. baking powder

1/2 t. salt
1 t. cinnamon
1/4 t. nutmeg
1/4 t. cloves

1. Preheat the oven to 350°.
2. Beat butter, honey, and eggs together.
3. Add buttermilk and mix well.
4. Mix dry ingredients together.
5. Add dry ingredients to wet ingredients and mix well.
6. Pour into a greased 9-inch cake pan and bake for 30 to 45 minutes.

Shared by Kirsten Carr ~
The Waldorf School, Lexington, Massachusetts

Gingerbread Men and Women

For Saint Nicholas day.

1/3 cup butter
2/3 cup honey
2/3 cup molasses
5 cups whole wheat flour
1-1/2 t. baking soda
1/2 t. cloves
1/2 t. cinnamon
3 t. ginger
1 t. salt

1. Preheat oven to 350°.
2. Blend the butter, honey, and molasses.
3. Sift the dry ingredients.
4. Add sifted ingredients to butter mixture.
5. If dough is too dry, add a little water or milk until dough forms a ball.
6. Chill for 1 hour if dough is sticky.
7. Roll out dough 1/4-inch thick.

8. Cut out gingerbread men and women.
9. Bake for 8 to 10 minutes.

Shared by Kirsten Carr ~
The Waldorf School, Lexington, Massachusetts

Thumbprint Oatmeal Cookies

For the Winter Garden (Advent Spiral). Makes 4 dozen cookies.

3 sticks of butter, softened
1 cup brown sugar
1 egg
1 t. vanilla
2-1/2 cups oats
2 cups flour
1/2 t. salt
1 cup raisins
1 cup chopped nuts (optional)
2/3 cup organic raspberry preserves

1. Preheat oven to 350°.
2. Cream butter and sugar until fluffy.
3. Add egg and vanilla, beating well.
4. In separate bowl, combine the dry ingredients, including the raisins and nuts (optional).
5. Add dry ingredients to wet ingredients and blend well.
6. Roll dough into 1-inch balls and place on ungreased cookie sheets.
7. Flatten balls slightly and make a thumb-print on each cookie. Fill thumbprints with preserves.
8. Bake for 15 to 20 minutes.

Shared by Heather Cohill ~
Waldorf School of Baltimore, Maryland

Rose Room Oatmeal Cookies

For the Lantern Walk. Contains no dairy or wheat!

1 cup margarine (or butter)
1-1/2 cups honey
1-1/2 cups maple syrup
4 bananas
1 can crushed pineapple
2 t. baking soda
1-1/2 t. baking powder
2 apples
1 cup oats
5 cups spelt flour (or wheat flour)
cinnamon
ginger

1. Mix melted margarine with honey and maple syrup.
2. In separate bowl, mash bananas, and then add pineapple, baking powder, and baking soda. Let sit until bubbly.
3. Grate apples and set aside.
4. Preheat oven to 350°.
5. In a large bowl, mix oats, flour, and spices. Then make a hole in the middle of these dry ingredients and pour in the honey/butter/syrup mixture. Stir.
6. Add banana/pineapple mixture and stir.
7. Add grated apples and stir. Mixture should be stiff but *not* dough-like.
8. Spoon onto oiled trays.
9. Bake for 10 to 15 minutes.

Shared by Denelle Diehl ~
Waldorf School of Baltimore, Maryland

Santa Lucia Buns

1/4 cup water
2 pkgs. yeast
2 cups warmed milk
1 egg
2 sticks butter, melted
1-1/4 cups sugar
8 cups flour
1-1/2 t. salt

1. In a large bowl, combine water and yeast. Allow to become foamy.
2. Mix together all ingredients, except butter.
3. Mix in butter.
4. Knead dough for 10 minutes.
5. Let rise for 1 hour.
6. Punch down dough.
7. Form into figure eight shapes. First make long, thin ropes. Then form into the figure eight shape or an S shape.
8. Brush egg whites on buns before baking.
9. Bake at 350° for 20 to 30 minutes.

Shared by Kirsten Carr ~
The Waldorf School, Lexington, Massachusetts

Ginger Snaps

A fun winter treat.

4 cups whole wheat flour
2 t. baking soda
1/2 cup butter
1-1/3 cups molasses
1 T. ginger
1 T. cinnamon
1/2 t. cloves

1. Preheat oven to 350°.
2. Mix all ingredients together, adding water if dough is too dry to form a large ball.
3. Roll dough into 1-inch balls.
4. Place on cookie sheet and bake for 10 to 15 minutes.

Shared by Kirsten Carr ~
The Waldorf School, Lexington, Massachusetts

Almond Butter Thumbprint Cookies

1/4 cup butter, softened
1/2 cup maple syrup
2/3 cup almond butter
1-1/3 cups whole wheat pastry flour
1 t. baking powder
1/3 t. salt
jam

1. Preheat oven to 350°.
2. Cream butter.
3. Mix in syrup.
4. Mix in almond butter.
5. Combine the dry ingredients. Then add them to wet ingredients and mix well.
6. Roll dough into balls and place on cookie sheet.
7. Press centers with thumb and fill the thumbprints with jam.
8. Bake for 12 minutes.

Shared by Kirsten Carr ~
The Waldorf School, Lexington, Massachusetts

Valentine Tarts

Makes about 13 3-inch heart tarts.

2-1/2 cups flour
1/3 cup sugar
1/4 t. baking soda
1/4 t. salt
1 egg
2 T. milk
2/3 cup butter (softened)
3/4 cup jam

1. Combine dry ingredients.
2. Add egg and milk and mix.
3. Mix the butter into the dough with your hands.
4. Knead it, adding flour if necessary to form a pliable, but not too sticky dough. You may refrigerate the dough at this point, if you wish.
5. Preheat oven to 350°.
6. Roll out dough on waxed paper, to about a 1/4-inch thickness.
7. Cut hearts. In half of them cut out a smaller heart in the middle.
8. Arrange the whole hearts on a greased cookie sheet. Place 1/2 T. of jam on the whole hearts, mostly in the middle, but spread it a bit, avoiding the edges.
9. Place hearts with a smaller cut-out heart on top of each whole heart.
10. Crimp the edges with a fork.
11. Bake for 10 to 15 minutes.

Shared by Lise Stoessel ~
Charlottesville Waldorf School, Virginia

Valentine Cookies

1/2 cup butter, softened
1/2 cup honey
1 egg
1/2 t. vanilla
1 1/2 cups flour
1/4 t. salt
1/4 t. baking powder
1 egg white
sugar for top of cookies (optional)

1. In a large bowl, beat together the butter, honey, egg, and vanilla.
2. Sift the flour, salt, and baking powder together and add to the bowl. Mix well.
3. Chill cookie dough for one hour.
4. Butter cookie sheets and preheat oven to 350°.
5. Roll dough to a 1/4 to 1/8-inch thickness and cut out hearts.
6. Brush with egg white and sprinkle with sugar (optional).
7. Bake for 8 minutes.

Shared by Kirsten Carr ~
The Waldorf School, Lexington, Massachusetts

Juicy Tea

A special festival beverage.

Wildberry Zinger tea (unsweetened)
Juice

Shared by Lise Stoessel ~
Charlottesville Waldorf School, Virginia

Irish Soda Bread

4 cups sifted flour
1/4 cup sugar
1 t. salt
1 t. baking powder
1/4 cup butter
2 cups raisins
1-1/3 cups buttermilk
1 egg, unbeaten
1 t. baking soda
1 egg yolk or a little cream

1. Preheat oven to 375°.
2. Grease a 2-quart casserole dish.
3. Sift flour, sugar, salt, and baking powder together.
4. With pastry blender, cut in softened butter until mixture is like coarse corn meal.
5. Stir in raisins.
6. In a separate bowl, combine the buttermilk, egg, and baking soda. Then stir into the flour mixture until moistened.
7. Turn dough onto a lightly floured board, kneading lightly until smooth.
8. Shape into a ball and place in casserole dish.
9. With a sharp knife, make a 4-inch cross, 1/4-inch deep, on the top of the ball.
10. Brush with a beaten egg yolk or cream.
11. Bake for 1 hour and 10 minutes.

Shared by Kirsten Carr ~
The Waldorf School, Lexington, Massachusetts

Sources

The following sources were referenced in this cookbook:

Fallon, Sally, with Enig, Mary G. Ph.D. *Nourishing Traditions*. Washington, DC: NewTrends Publishing, Inc., 2001.

Glöckler, Michaela. *Education as Preventive Medicine: A Salutogenic Approach*. Trans. Maria St. Goar and Uwe Stave. Fair Oaks, CA: Rudolf Steiner College Press, 2002.

Glöckler, Michaela and Goebel, Wolfgang. *A Guide to Child Health*. Trans. Polly Lawson. Edinburgh: Floris Books, 1990.

Graf, Emma. *Cooking with Grains*. Trans. Richard and Maia Brinton. Stroud, UK: InterActions, 1996.

Salter, Joan. *The Incarnating Child*. Gloucestershire, UK: Hawthorn Press, 1987.

About the Author

Lisa Hildreth holds an M.S. in Ed. in Waldorf Early Childhood Education and an M.A. in English. After spending a decade as a technical writer in the computer industry, she learned of Rudolf Steiner and Anthroposophy. She is currently a kindergarten teacher at the Susquehanna Waldorf School. Lisa lives in Lancaster, Pennsylvania, with her husband, Arthur, and sons, David and Robert.

About the Illustrator

Jo Valens teaches kindergarten at the Rudolf Steiner School in Great Barrington, Massachusetts. She lives in Great Barrington with her husband and has a beautiful garden where she loves to work and draw and seek communion with the elemental world.

Index